I will follow Zulfiya
(Poetry & Prose)

By:
Oringaliyeva Nurjayna Orazgaliyevna

© Taemeer Publications LLC
I will follow Zulfiya *(Poetry & Prose)*
by: Oringaliyeva Nurjayna Orazgaliyevna
Edition: August '2023
Publisher:
Taemeer Publications LLC (Michigan, USA / Hyderabad, India)

© Taemeer Publications

Book	:	*I will follow Zulfiya (Poetry & Prose)*
Author	:	**Oringaliyeva Nurjayna Orazgaliyevna**
Publisher	:	Taemeer Publications
Year	:	'2023
Pages	:	56
Title Design	:	*Taemeer Web Design*

Table of Content

Poetry

- I will follow Zulfiya
- You are great, my Karakalpak
- My Uzbekistan
- My heavenly country, my Uzbekistan
- My songs are for my country
- Homeland
- Grandfather Ibrahim
- My Uzbek language
- Be a follower of Zulfiyakhanim
- My unsaid truths
- 2013
- My grandmother
- My school
- To President Shavkat Mirziyoyev
- May your face always be bright
- Your childhood is your wealth
- Brave soldiers of my country
- Young people of new Uzbekistan
- Don't make my mother cry
- My teacher

Prose

- My mother is my pride
- The age of innocence
- My country Uzbekistan is on the way to development
- My favorite newspaper
- Motherland
- I am proud of my mother
- Education
- Knowledge brings happiness
- Who did the right thing?
- A story from my childhood
- "I will be a soldier"
- A book is an incomparable wealth
- Consequence

Oringaliyeva Nurjayna Orazgaliyevna was born on November 11, 2006 in Nukus, Republic of Karakalpakstan. Currently, she is an 11th grade Russian student of school 37 in Nukus. Author of the book 'Maktabim-fakhrim'. The winner of the school, city and republic stages of the Uzbek language Olympiad. Winner of the 1st place in the contest 'Young Reader' held by the Ministry of Public Education of Uzbekistan and the Federation of Trade Unions of Uzbekistan. She won the 1st place in the school, city and republic stages of essay contests. 'Words in the heart' and 'World of new talents' were published in English by 'Just Fiction Edition' publishing house in the European city of Moldava, 'Çiçekler' was published in Turkish, 'Flowers from the bud' were published in Uzbek, and 'From the Diary of Daisies' in the international anthologies 'Mir glazami jenshchiny' published by the Russian Federation 'Slovo serdtsa' publishing house. The articles, poems and stories of the young artist are published in the republican 'Jetkinshek', 'Korakalpakistan Tong', 'Ezgulik', 'Bekajon' newspapers and 'Uzbekistanda Talim' magazine. Member of the international organizations 'All India Council for Technical Skill Development' and 'National Human Rights and Humanitarian Federation' of India. She was awarded the 'Altin Qiran' medal of the 'Double Wing' Foundation of the Republic of Kazakhstan and the 'Talent' commemorative badge for her cooperation with the 'Education in Uzbekistan' magazine and her talent and achievements in the field of artistic creativity. Today, as a member of the 'Khalk donoligi' folklore club under the Writers' Union of Karakalpakstan, and the 'Young Artists' circle under the Union and the 'Amudarya' magazine, she actively participates in public and promotional work.

I will follow Zulfiya

Always honest, dear, holy,
Our hearts are filled with pride.
The sun of literature shines,
Uzbek poet Zulfiyakhanim.

Swallowed the pain of longing,
Only people expected justice.
The whole life has been faithful,
Zulfiyakhanim, the symbol of loyalty.

The poems she wrote are our inheritance,
To generations to come.
She says, "My son, there will be end the war."
Zulfiyakhanim says that she lived in my country.

My dream, my wish is to be like you
To justify the trust of the president.
May God help me and follow you,
I will achieve my dream, Zulfiyakhanim.

I will be a fire like Zulfiyakhanim.
I will follow Zulfiyakhanim!

You are great, my Karakalpak

If he speaks, stay away from the words of the fat people,

Light shines from his laughing eyes.

He compares his face to an angel,

My Karakalpak, with matching coats.

Wherever I go, call me Karakalpak girl.

As the trail of Kunkhoja, Berdak, Alakoz.

As the shining face and eyes of this nation,

My Karakalpak, whom I created.

Peaceful, beautiful countryside, cities,

A place that grandfathers dreamed of.

So there is a rule of the country, tell me, where is it?

Ibrayim Baba's land is Karakalpak.

The people of this space are loyal,

He may have affection for Kyrgyz, Turkmen, and Uzbek.

The direction is clear, the path is always bright,

Karakalpag, where "Aydinlar" went to the world.

He works for the good fortune of our country,

He sacrificed his life for our country.

The Creator Himself sustains us,

"Beshbarmak" is made Karakalpak.

It's like I came into this world with happiness,

I will always keep your peace.

I rejoice every day,

The land of paradise, Karakalpak.

My Uzbekistan

Why don't I explain to you?
My space, which is valuable for everyone.
My country, your name is rising day by day,
My umbilical cord blood dripped Uzbekistan.

If I write you, my sweet soul will rest
You have raised Ulugbek, Mirzo Babur.
You feel unparalleled pride like Navoi,
My real happiness is Uzbekistan.

Your song will not leave my tongue, my memory,
Indescribable language, level like the sea.
Shame on you, my soul, your unknown value,
Your sons and daughters are the crown, my Uzbekistan.

You are great, you are as high as the sky,
I sing, I am a swan, and you are humming.
If you're sorry, come to us.

My heavenly country, my Uzbekistan.

I will raise your flag to the skies,

I will introduce you to the whole world.

You won't leave my heart even for a second

May you live forever, my Uzbekistan.

My songs are for my country

I am happy, a child of this peaceful land.

I am a daughter of a kind mother.

My flights are starting, look, today

My thanks are for my country.

The thorn in my heel is liquid,

Every daughter and son praises you.

I respect this country, why?

My thanks are only for my country.

When a guest comes, our people go out to the roads,

They do not separate.

Five goes to sweet children,

I say "Thank you" for the Motherland.

Whatever is sown will grow everywhere.

I describe your definition in every poem.

Nurjayna always studies

My thanks, you know, are only for my country.

Homeland

I was born in an independent country,

The soil is in a sacred space.

Instills pride in every person,

This is the best Motherland that the world envies!

Thank you for all these days,

There are many brave and brave children in this country,

These prosperous days are precious days,

Our people say a thousand thanks every morning.

Live until the world stops, mother

You are my crown and Kaaba,

The dearest person in the world to me,

Your heart is full of goodness,

Live until the world stops, mother.

You are always burning as my child,

You gave me love with white milk,

She taught me everything if I make a mistake,

Live until the world stops, mother.

You are my sun and my moon.
You are my dear, my most precious thing,
My angel, my dear, my only wish:
Live until the world stops, mother.

Grandfather Ibrahim
(In memory of the People's Poet of Karakalpakstan Ibrayim Yusupov)

Your name was our pride,

Our beloved grandfather.

You will not leave my heart,

Awake in hearts, Grandpa Ibrayim.

Every word you say starts moving forward

You are the true poet of Karakalpak,

We still remember your bright eyes,

The poet of Karakalpak, grandfather Ibrayim.

My Uzbek language

From the great ancestors
My heritage.
Have your place in the world
My tongue sounds loud.

He gave Alisher a pen.
His ghazals have reached the world.
Envied by the whole world,
I am proud of my Uzbek language.

My mother, thank you very much
(To my mother Elmira Shamshetova)

You did not do less and grew again,
Don't eat yourself, just feed me.
I thank you, mother,
Let your eyes be happy when you see me.

You always see the good,
My treasure is my infinite wealth.

I thank you, mother,

I need you in this world.

It's okay to laugh if it's you,

Even wearing clothes made of chit or silk.

I thank you, mother,

There is no sorrow in your heart.

They say mother's prayer,

Pray, be a wise child.

Everyone as they wish,

Be a follower of Zulfiyakhanim.

I'm happy, know, only with you

I am a person who does not know stinginess.

I thank you, mother,

The words are kind, sweet, kind.

My unsaid truths

Dad...
I did not mention this word at all.
I've been thinking about it for seventeen years.
I am writing this poem with dreams,
To the person I left when I was a baby.

Dad...
Why did you hate it?
Tell me what is my sin.
How much I suffered, how much!
God alone is my witness.

You weren't even interested in me
You didn't ask about my condition.
Why did you leave us?
So I have only one question for you.

When I opened my eyes, it was my grandmother,
She was always petting me.
Only my mother was with me.
You didn't even ask me how I was.

2013

September dawned.

Grandma woke me up early in the morning.

I put a book and bread in my bag,

I took the first step towards the school.

If I write down the letters my grandmother told me,

My teacher always praised me.

If I tell you the verses of Navoi,

She used to say "Scientist Nurjayna".

I wanted to play in the street

But they did not join me, children.

Why should I say to me: "You don't have a father"

They were laughing at me.

I always greeted my friends,

They couldn't help but look at me.

I was watching alone at one corner,

I know they didn't like me at all.

I remember...

March 5, 2017

There was no end to my joys,

Maybe the person I see in the picture-

My father came to see me.

No, I was wrong.

You sent your son to my school,

While you are sitting, waiting for you to come out.

If I look quietly at one end,

You are leaving, holding your son's hand.

The next day I saw you again,

There is sadness in my heart, sometimes pain, sometimes sadness.

I went to you because I am a daugther,

If I go, you don't even know me.

I told these things to my grandmother and mother.

I know that they cried without realizing it.

Even if they laugh at me, they swallow it

Sufferings pierced their hearts and minds.

That day I set a goal for myself-

"I will be a worthy child for my grandmother

"Thank you to your grandmother and mother"

I will make them hear the word.

It's a dream come true to say that I have a father,

Unfortunately, my grandmother passed away early.

Look, dad, the world is strange.

Today they told me: "Thank your father."

Thank my mother and grandmother.

They don't eat themselves, they only feed me,

Those who always see goodness,

Their eyes are always happy to see me.

The day will come when I will conquer a great goal.

Having a mother is my true happiness,

I thank her a thousand times.

My mother is my pride, my mother is my crown, my mother is my throne.

Lucky days await me I'm taking a step forward to my future.

Victories come by the hand

This suits me, this is how I live.

I am my mother's dream and hope.

I always get strength from your prayers.

God willing, God willing,

I make my mother the happiest woman.

My grandmother
(In memory of my grandmother Kalligul Shamshetova)

When he turned away from me, my father

You were with me when I was born.

You've been a blessing to me, grandma

Sometimes when I cry.

Both my great-grandmother and my father,

She was happy to see my achievements.

You said, "these days will pass, daughter"

"My daughter," she said from the bottom of her heart.

I haven't found a person like you in the world.

She didn't think about me for a moment.

Always call me grandma,

"My dear girl, be happy," she said.

Your name is our pride,

Kindness and desire did not fade from her heart.

My achievements were your happiness,

You were kind, everyone needs it.

Even if her heart is full of pain,

My grandmother was the kindest grandmother.

Even if they are sick

Thinking of me, she sometimes cried and sometimes laughed.

Your name was our pride,

You are my inexhaustible wealth, grandmother.

May God make your place in Paradise,

My grandmother is my dear, my dear.

We enjoyed your prayers.

Grandma, we're getting late without you.

But we lost our great wealth.

Grandma, we miss you.

You would give me the greatest wealth,

Your words will not leave my ears.

Life is just a moment.

No one knows what will happen next.

I am amazed at your patience,

I will be a worthy child for you.

God willing, God willing,
I always move forward in life.

You have grown, do not do less than anyone,
Thank you, my kind grandmother.
Don't forget the merit of your life,
God bless you, grandmother.

Running around saying only me
Your work is always worth it.
Studying day and night,
I am a follower of Zulfiyakhanim.

My school

Hello, my dear school,

My beloved, my bright sun.

Giving the heart the light of knowledge,

The sun is shining, my school.

May the morning be bright –

You have set a goal.

Calling us every day.

You gave us knowledge.

Kind like my mother,

My gardener in the garden of knowledge.

I am like the sun,

My school is bright.

They got knowledge from you

How great, clever people.

You made them a scientist.

My bright school.

To President Shavkat Mirziyoyev

You are gone, we live in peaceful times,
The door of opportunities is open for us.
The soil is sacred in this great Motherland
We bring thanks just for you.

You are introducing the Uzbek nation to the world.
Always doing all the merits.
You are focusing on the younger generation,
We are all reading a book today.

How happy are the children today?!
A person who gives goodness to the heart.
Our people only trust you,
You are lucky to be alive.

You will not be found in any country –
He gave so many opportunities to young people.
My motherland, my people, can't even sleep,
He loved our country more than his life.

We are happy today because of you

We are growing up not knowing why war.

You are our mountain, you are a great maple.

May your face always be bright.

You make the country bloom, the garden and the garden,

A happy future awaits us.

You miss Uzbekistan every day.

Our country will become world famous.

We deserve your trust,

Our desire is only for the future.

Always seeing joy in your eyes,

The younger generation will always show their strength.

My dear mother

You filled my eyes with light like the sun,

You have satisfied me from the fountain of love,

Grown without straining,

I bow to you, dear mother.

When I rejoice, you rejoice like children,

You gave education and upbringing,

My child burned because of me,

I bow to you, dear mother.

You are the creator of your heart,
You are the reason for my happy days,
I am happy that you are always healthy.
You are my wealth, my loving mother.

Your childhood is your wealth

Childhood is a beautiful bird,
The most expensive of all time.
This is wealth, this is dream,
This is a picture of heaven.

Homeland-free, Homeland-prosperous
Blooming day by day.
You have friends cheerful, joyful
These are the real riches for you.

You're playing hide and seek
Only peace in our country.
There is joy and happiness everywhere
Isn't that what wealth is all about?

Look around: air, water and bread,
You see the world, your existence.
Your parents are safe and sound.
Your childhood is your wealth.

Brave soldiers of my country

Thinking about the future of the country,
Unbent, never broken,
May they live long for the country,
Brave, brave soldiers of country.

Loyalty learned from grandfathers,
Always in the service of the country,
"My life is sacrificed for my country," they said
Brave, soldiers of my country.

You are worthy of the Motherland,
I admit, You are not afraid of enemies, of any evil,
You fight the enemy to the death,
Brave, boys of my country.

Young people of new Uzbekistan

Striving for the future of the country,
Fulfilling the duty to the Motherland.
They always show their strength-
The proud youth of New Uzbekistan.

The sky is clear, there is peace on this earth
Unyielding their proud heads.
They read and study
Wise young people of New Uzbekistan.

In all competitions in every direction
Raise the flag of the Motherland in the sky.
The great way is in the tracks and the search
Happy young people of New Uzbekistan.

Quickly steps towards goals,
They have unlimited opportunities.
Let's introduce our country to the world,
Dear young people of New Uzbekistan.

Don't make my mother cry

If only the great one would laugh,
The whole world will prosper.
Calling another child "You are my child".
She gives them love, happiness, joy.

Always wishes everyone health:
"Let there be evil in this world.
May there always be peace, safety,
Let everyone do good to each other."

Then you went to bad dreams
Actually, you made a big mistake.
Are you interested in those things?
Now you know you were wrong.

Her heart is full of joy,
If she cries, it will be a river of tears.
All you have left is a memory
You didn't know, after all, this is another world.

She spares everything for you

Don't forget the past days.

I have only one request for you:

Don't make my mother cry anymore.

My teacher
(To my teacher Mirturdi Dosnazarov)

How can I describe it to you?

You are the one who has hurt me in my heart,

Knowledge shines in your heart,

It always flowed like water.

Thank you, my dear teacher

My gardener in the science garden.

I bow down to you.

Good luck, my teacher.

We are not your disciples, but your children,

How many years have you worked hard?

They invite us to knowledge like the sun,

The heart of a river is without a person, my dear teacher.

"The teacher is as great as your father," they say

My word in my heart is only for you.

I want to be a teacher like you

You are a disciple, my teacher.

Enjoy how many years of hard work,

My teacher, we bow to you.

God, face the hundred years,

Do not rush to teach, my teacher.

My mother is my pride

My grandmother, that is, my mother's mother Kalligul Shamshetova, worked as a teacher in the kindergarten. My mother, Elmira Shamshetova, envied her mother and currently works in kindergarten number 6 in our capital. She loves children very much. Even if she is tired after looking after so many children at work, she makes time for me. She always help me prepare lessons and take care of me. Almost all the children raised by my mother studied at higher educational institutions and became people who contribute to the development of our country. She is very happy when her children come to look for her during the holidays. At such times, I love to see my mother. She is kind people who loved not only us, but many children. I am proud of my mother. I hope you are always healthy, my mother!

The age of innocence

Nature looks very beautiful in winter, especially when it snows. The trees, the autumn leaves-everything turns white. The streets, where children play dusty in the summer also look clean in the winter. When I was a child, I strongly believed in Santa Claus. I still remember that time, I was 7 years old. This year, winter came very cold. We celebrated the New Year on December 31. I wrote a letter to Santa that night. In my letter, I wished Santa a happy holiday and asked him to bring me a present, including chocolates, my favorite cookies, and some other things. Then I put this letter under my pillow and fell asleep. The next morning, when I got up early and took my pillow, I found that I had not written a letter. It's a gift if it's next to the TV, it has everything I wrote inside. And my joy has no limit: "What if... What if Santa Claus came to our house?!" After the winter break, I went to school and told all my friends what had happened. To tell the truth, they did not believe that there was a Santa Claus. But I wrote a letter to Santa every year. Before going to bed at night, I would write in a letter what he would bring me, and the next day I would have everything I asked for. It was an incident from my childhood, when I was innocent. It always reminds me of the New Year holiday. Later I found out that my grandmother Kalligul and my mother Elmira bought my writings to cheer me up.

My country Uzbekistan is on the way to development

In recent years, our motherland, Uzbekistan, has undergone great changes in every field. Starting from our beautiful city of Nukus, wide paved streets, beautiful, modern houses, buildings, kindergartens and schools are being built in the remotest villages of our republic. In order to add joy to the joy of village children and spend their free time meaningfully, sports fields were built. Libraries have taken place in a special way for book-loving students. I study in the 11th Russian class of the 37th general education school in our capital. Nowadays, many opportunities have been created for us, the youth. Our President put forward five initiatives to support the youth. My little brother Atabek participates in wrestling at the Children's sports complex in Karaozak district, and in athletics in Hurliman. They always rave about the conditions here. So, our heavenly country is developing day by day. Our neighbors and friends are representatives of different nationalities. We live peacefully with them. If we all serve as one force in the development of our country, we will definitely move forward. Therefore, I will contribute to the comprehensive development of our motherland by studying well. Come, friends, let's all unite and serve our Motherland!

My favorite newspaper

91 years ago, on January 20, 1932, "Jetkinshek" newspaper was published. Despite his age, he was a confidant and friend of children and called them to maturity. I have also been an active reporter for the newspaper for many years. I rush to the editor's office every week to get a new issue of the newspaper. My mother helps me subscribe to the newspaper whenever she can. "Jetkinshek" newspaper publishes various stories, poems, interesting creative works of my peers. I would like to thank my mother who brought me to the editorial office for the first time. Now I am not only reading the newspaper, I am doing my own work. I also read the newspaper during the winter vacation. "Jetkinshek" will remain my favorite newspaper and I wish "Jetkinshek" has a bright future. I believe that it will remain a childrens' favorite newspaper even after centuries.

Motherland

Today we had a history lesson. I love this lesson very much, because our teacher Matyakubov Orinbai tells interesting stories and poems in every lesson. Once upon a time there lived two kings. The first was very quarrelsome and the second was very kind. The quarrelsome king hated the kind king so much that he was looking for an excuse to quarrel. The quarrelsome king asked his neighbor for gold, a camel and a dagger. The kind king agreed and gave gold, a camel and a dagger. In order to fight again, he asked him for a place where no one lives. But this time he did not agree. After all, the small land of the Motherland is also the Motherland.

Motherland is dear, sacred. Not even a piece of it is given. Each of us should protect our Motherland.

I am proud of my mother

I learned many good qualities from my mother. My mother is a very honest, hardworking, simple woman. Although my mother did not tell me the concepts of respect for elders and honor for children, I learned from her actions and words because I spent a lot of time with her. Ever since I was a child, wherever my mother went, I loved to go with her. I would hold my mother's hands with my small hands and look around. Nature seemed very mysterious to me. At that time, I thought that the characters I had read about in fairy-tale books would suddenly appear in front of me.In the books, good characters are depicted so wonderfully that I even dreamed of living in the same house with them. Because they are very good, honest, always help the people who come before them. That's why I read fairy tales and stories. In the evenings, if I can't sleep, I take the books that my mother brought me and go to my grandmother and sit on her lap. My mother and I go to the market and buy toys for myself and my little brother. On one of those days, my mother and I went to the market. That day, I woke up early and helped my mother with the housework in order to go to the market earlier. After cleaning the house, we headed to the market with my mother holding a bag in one hand and me in the other. My mother would think of something, and I would watch the mysterious nature as if we were waiting for the heroes of fairy tales to appear in front of us. The only thing in my mind is this: if a fairy-tale hero appeared in front of us, I would have told my mother about him and taken him home for a day. We got things from the market to take home, groceries, cookies that I love, toys for my little brother, and a few other things. Even though we bought so many things, my mother couldn't buy anything for herself. As we pass by the sisters who sell scarves, we ask: "Can't you buy a scarf?" – she kept shouting after us. When I said to my mother: "Let's get you a scarf," she looked at me and laughed without words. On our way back home from the market, our bags became heavy because of our many things. Together with my mother, we stopped and walked along the road. After a hot day, when I was thirsty and drinking water , a sister who was one year older and lived next door came to us. "She must be coming from the market too," I thought. She was struggling to lift his bag. Seeing this, my mother immediately took her bag from the sister's hand, even though her bag was heavy. She thanked my mother before saying that she would come home. While entering the house, she stopped for a while and blessed my mother. At that time, I saw my mother who rushed to help others despite her heavy bag. When I grow up, I want to be a good, loving person like my mother. On this day, I did not meet the heroes of fairy tales, but I came with a heroine. Yes, my mother is my hero.

Education

Being an only child in his home, Andrew grew up to be quite a man. He would not do what he was told, his sisters would not shout at him, and his parents would bring up his masculinity and whims because he was still small. Time passed, but Andrew's masculinity and whims increased, but did not decrease at all. At school, he made a mess and was reprimanded by his teachers. No matter how much he called for order, he would not hide from what he knew. Today, a classmate got into a fight with his friend and heard from the principal. Andrew, who came out in front of the director, went straight home without looking anywhere. He didn't even answer his teacher's questions while leaving the class. He did not even know that he came home with different thoughts. His mother was waiting in the kitchen, preparing food for him. Brave kicked open the door of his house and entered his room. Without even changing his clothes, he took his phone in his hand and indulged in the game. Then, feeling that he was hungry, he took a piece of bread from the table, ate it as he went, and stepped on it with his feet. He did not even notice that it was late sitting in this position. In the meantime, the school director called Andrew's father and asked him to come to school. The director started the conversation from a distance, and at the end he touched on what Andrew had done and said that if it is not prevented, it will be too late. In fact, Andrew's father, who noticed that Andrew had changed a lot, felt that it was impossible to talk to his son properly. Of course, the father, who apologized to the director for what his son had done, hurried to go home as soon as possible. When he came, Andrew did not appear at the table. Andrew reluctantly came after sending several times to his elder sister: "Call Andrew." When he came, he sat with his phone in his hand. His father started questioning Andrew. At first, he said that he was disorderly in today's school, that he was getting bad grades in classes, and that he apologized to the principal. "Bring your diary," said his father. Out of desperation, Andrew brought his diary and gave it to his father. In several subjects, the grade "2" was given to the diary. The father began to regret that he had pampered his son a lot. Then he told Andrew that he would not give him his phone anymore, that he would change "2" to "5" in his diary. In the meantime, Andrew's school was shown on television and the achievements of his neighbor Jack were mentioned. Seeing this situation, Andrew was ashamed and both his faces turned red. Andrew apologized to his parents, sisters and teachers and promised to change for the better and study well. After that Andrew changed, he was the first to apologize to his friends. He made a habit of attending classes and completing assignments on time. This year, he won the Science Olympiad and was lucky enough to be a student without exams. When he remembers his childhood masculinity, whims, and deeds, he is ashamed of himself and expresses his endless gratitude to his father for showing him the right path. His relatives are proud of his achievements.

Knowledge brings happiness

I love my grandmother very much. She always tells me interesting, useful information, instructive stories from each other. Today after dinner I went to my room. My grandmother came to my room and told me a very interesting story: Many years ago, Jane and Ann studied in the same class. Jane is very rich, she wears different clothes every day, her father was a businessman. Although Ann has no clothes to wear except her school uniform, she actively participates in classes and gets excellent grades. Jane always laughed at Ann and gossiped about her, hated to study, even though her teachers reprimanded her, she never studied. Years have passed. They graduated from school and never saw or talked to each other. Meanwhile, Jane's parents left this bright world due to an accident. Jane did not study anywhere, she married a businessman. As for Ann, she was lucky enough to graduate with a gold medal and become a student without exams. Jane's husband got into trouble and ended up selling everything in his house. Now Jane had nothing left but one piece of clothing. At that moment, Jane was very sorry for laughing at her friend Ann while studying at school. The next day, when Jane was looking for work on the street, a beautiful girl who looked like Ann walked out in front of him. Jane: "Isn't this Ann?" When she was hesitating, the student coming out of the school said: "Hello, teacher Ann". Jane immediately ran and introduced herself to her. At first, Ann did not recognize Jane, because Jane was wearing expensive clothes, and her face had no wrinkles. Ann told the events that happened to Jane and asked her friend for forgiveness for all the bad things she did to her, for gossiping and laughing at her. I learned from this story told by my grandmother. Laughing at someone, gossiping is a very bad habit. Because this is another world...

Who did the right thing?

It was one of the autumn days. As usual, the girls coming from school were talking to each other. High-class schoolgirls used to tell others what happened at home and what they heard from their mother. Among them was a girl named Sarah, who did not agree with what her friends said, attended her classes regularly, and studied well. Probably because Sarah was brought up by her grandmother or because she read a lot of books, she often quoted proverbs. The girls started talking about tomorrow's day off. Someone suggested going to the market, someone suggested going for ice cream. Everyone tried to do what she said. Jane, who was among them, said that she would go to the village and help her grandmother in harvesting the sugarcane crops. Then Anastasia looked at her friends: "Let's go for a spin," she said. "Okay," Jerry agreed. Sarah, who was listening to them, did not like what her friends said. Because she has other plans, she doesn't know how to tell her friends. How to say? On her way to study, her neighbor Emma, who lives alone on the street, saw the garbage around the house and collected it as much as he could. She started studying and preparing for the Science Olympiad, and did not have time to find out about sister Emma. Sarah, coming with these thoughts, began to speak slowly: - Better, let's go to sister Emma's house on our street and help her with the housework. It would be a reward if the yard and the streets were cleaned, if the old people were informed about their condition. You know, sister Emma lives alone at home, I heard from my grandmother that she is sick. It would be nice if we could help with the housework, girls... – Let's go to the cinema instead, - said one of the girls. This word was liked by other girls. With such thoughts, the girls went home. Jane came home and went with her parents to the village, to her grandmother's house. Sarah came home and told her mother about her plans for tomorrow. Hearing this, her mother was very happy and hugged her daughter. Take your brothers with you, my daughter, you think very well, each of us should do meritorious deeds every day, - her mother started to have dinner. Having finished her breakfast, Sarah took her brothers and went to sister Emma's house. She gave the gifts that her mother had given to the owner of the house and started doing things herself. Firstly she cleaned the house, then she went out and started cleaning the surroundings of the house. Sister Emma was happy to see this. As for Sarah's other friends went to the cinema and saw a movie there. In the meantime, Anastasia lost her new phone that her father brought her in the market, and Jerry lost her money. No matter how hard they both searched, they couldn't find what they lost. In the evening, when they were coming home, Sarah and her brothers were returning from doing sister Emma's housework. Sister Emma repeatedly thanked Sarah and her brothers and blessed them. Seeing this, Anastasia and Jerry were very ashamed. They agreed not to go on such tours anymore, to help single people and families in need. Sister Emma went to school the next day and expressed her gratitude to Sarah and thanked her parents and teachers. Teachers showed Sarah as an example to other students and explained that it is necessary to do such meritorious deeds.

A story from my childhood

It goes without saying that the period of going to school is special for all children. When I remember my childhood, I remember the interesting events that happened during my school days. We played a lot of interesting games with the children. It was very interesting that we did our lessons with children. My mother took me to school in the 1st grade. I didn't want to go to school because I was a girl who didn't come from the game when I was little. On the first day, I cried "I can't stay at school" because I thought we would stay at school with the kids. Mom said, "I'll take it now." Our first teacher is very kind. She never yells at children. She explains what we don't know. She explained in an interesting way about nature, the mother earth we live on, our Motherland, the knowledge that should be taught in school. I was ready to stay at school on the first day because I liked school. Now when I say school, the first thing that comes to my mind is my kind teacher with a smiling face, the children who rush to school, the dear garden of my school that greets us in the morning. On the first day, after the lessons, when I went out to say goodbye to our teacher and the children whom I met today, but who have become dear, my sister Sayora was waiting for me. On the way home, I told my sister Sayora about the interesting events that happened at school today, about our teacher. My grandmother was worried about me at home when she saw that I was crying because I would not go to school in the morning. As soon as I entered the house, I ran to hug my grandmother and happily told her about our school. My grandmother, who saw my happiness, listened carefully to what I said with a surprised and happy face. Then she laughed and asked me: "So, are you going to school now?". If I look closely, our first teacher looks a lot like my grandmother. The next day, I got up early before my mother to go to school. My passion for reading increased day by day so that we could learn new interesting information every day at school. Now, when we sit with our family, when my mother tells me that I don't go to school, we all laugh.

"I will be a soldier"

My brother Atabek is six years old. Atabek Polatov is a pupil of kindergarten number 2 in Karaozak district. He is very smart. In particular, he asks a lot of interesting questions. One day he saw soldiers on TV and asked a question.

- Sister, what do the soldiers do, why are they carrying a machine gun? – he said.

- Soldiers are the guards of the Motherland. They will be strong, energetic young men. They protect and strengthen our borders in the mountains, rocks and water. I said that because of the presence of soldiers, mother, me, you, your father, your mother, we all live peacefully.

- Sister, then I will also become a soldier in the future. "I will protect my parents and my country," he stood up. After that day, he asked his parents to get him a soldier's uniform. Now he puts on a soldier's uniform and says to the guest who came to the house: "I will be a soldier!" he says. I am happy with what little Atabek has done. I wish that his future intention will come true and he will become a soldier.

A book is an incomparable wealth

Sister Liz loves to read books. For this reason, every evening when she returns from work, her son buys a book and brings it to Jack. Jack is very happy to read them. After reading, he tells his mother about the book. Today, sister Liz brought her son Jack Abdulla Kadiri's book "The Past". The book is very interesting. The more Jack reads about the lives of the heroes of this work, he wanted to read more. Days passed. Jack did not have time to read the end of the work because he had time to go to school. Jack thought: "I will read my book during the school break" and took the book away. The first lesson was mathematics. Jack went to the board and solved the examples correctly and received a grade of "5". Because he reads a lot of books, he gets excellent grades in all subjects. It was 45 minutes before the class started and the bell rang. Jack immediately took his book and started reading. At that moment, his classmate Ann saw the book in Jack's hand. – What kind of book is this? Ann asked. "This is Abdulla Kadiri's novel "Gone Days", Jack answered. After that, Ann asked him to give the book for a day. At first Jack did not agree, because he did not give his books to anyone. After Ann asked for the book, Jack agreed to give it only for one day. Three days passed. And Ann has not come to school for three days. Not knowing what to do next, Jack was coming home from school when Ann left. Jack explained that while asking Ann for his book, his brother tore it up. Hearing this, Jack got angry and said to Ann: "Why are you giving the book to your brother? After all, the price of this book was expensive". Jack did not know how he went home thinking about the book. When he entered the house, his mother was preparing food for him. Both Jack's faces turned red and shyly told his mother what had happened. Hearing this, his mother replied to her son: "Don't be upset, my son. The value of the book is not in its money, but in the fact that it has been read a lot." Then sister Liz went to the bookstore and bought one more book for her son Jack.

Consequence

One day, a deer was hungry in the forest and was looking for food. When Zebra, Giraffe, Rabbit, Monkey and other friends asked, they said they were hungry and had nothing to eat. After that, hunters saw a deer walking alone in the forest. Seeing this, the deer immediately hid behind a tree. The hunters did not see where he went. While they were going back, the deer started eating the leaves of the tree. When the hunters returned, the deer was standing behind a leafless tree. They shot the deer. The arrow hit the deer and the animal died.

What do you guys think? Is what the deer did right?

www.ingramcontent.com/pod-product-compliance
Lightning Source LLC
LaVergne TN
LVHW010618070526
838199LV00063BA/5194